Moments Together

for

WEATHERING LIFE'S STORMS

DENNIS and BARBARA RAINEY

Regal

From Gospel Light
Ventura, California, U.S.A.

Regal

PUBLISHED BY REGAL BOOKS
FROM GOSPEL LIGHT
VENTURA, CALIFORNIA, U.S.A.
PRINTED IN THE U.S.A.

Regal Books is a ministry of Gospel Light, a Christian publisher dedicated to serving the local church. We believe God's vision for Gospel Light is to provide church leaders with biblical, user-friendly materials that will help them evangelize, disciple and minister to children, youth and families.

It is our prayer that this Regal book will help you discover biblical truth for your own life and help you meet the needs of others. May God richly bless you.

For a free catalog of resources from Regal Books/Gospel Light, please call your Christian supplier or contact us at 1-800-4-GOSPEL or www.regalbooks.com.

Rights for publishing this book in other languages are contracted by Gospel Light Worldwide, the international non-profit ministry of Gospel Light. Gospel Light Worldwide also provides publishing and technical assistance to international publishers dedicated to producing Sunday School and Vacation Bible School curricula and books in the languages of the world. For additional information, visit www.gospellightworldwide.org; write to Gospel Light Worldwide, P.O. Box 3875, Ventura, CA 93006; or send an e-mail to info@gospellightworldwide.org.

All Scripture quotations are taken from the *New American Standard Bible,* © 1960, 1962, 1963, 1968, 1971, 1972, 1973, 1975, 1977 by The Lockman Foundation. Used by permission.

Some material taken from *Staying Close* by Dennis Rainey, Word Publishing, 1989. Used by permission from Word Publishing.

Some material taken from *The New Building Your Mate's Self-Esteem* by Dennis and Barbara Rainey, Thomas Nelson Publishers, 1995. Used by permission from Thomas Nelson Publishers.

The publisher regrets the omission of credits and requests documentation for future printings.

Cover and interior design by Robert Williams
Edited by Stephanie Parrish and Dave Boehi

Library of Congress Cataloging-in-Publication Data

Rainey, Dennis, 1948–
   Moments together for weathering life's storms / Dennis and Barbara Rainey.
        p.   cm.
   Includes bibliographical references and index.
   ISBN 0-8307-3329-9
   1.   Christian life—Meditations. 2.   Christian life—Anecdotes.   I. Rainey, Barbara. II. Title.
BV4832.3 .R35 2004
242'.4—dc22   2003009737

1   2   3   4   5   6   7   8   9   /   09   08   07   06   05   04   03

INTRODUCTION

Faith makes a family work. It's the active ingredient. It's the catalyst that causes you to implement biblical principles in your family relationships, trusting God to use your obedience to build oneness.

Many people, however, would find it difficult to give a true biblical definition of "faith." Some people use the word almost as a substitute for "belief," as in "I am part of the Christian faith, while my neighbor is part of the Muslim faith." And cynical secularists claim that believing in Christ involves a blind "leap of faith."

We like the definition of "faith" provided by our friend Ney Bailey in her book *Faith Is Not a Feeling;* she says that faith is simply taking God at His word: "God's Word is truer than anything I feel. God's Word is truer than anything I experience. God's Word is truer than any circumstances I will ever face. God's Word is truer than anything in the world."[1] That's what the writer of Hebrews meant when he described faith as "the assurance of things hoped for, the conviction of things not seen" (Heb. 11:1). Faith is not blind hope that is thrown to the wind. Rather, it is a growing confidence, based on the knowledge that God and His Word are true.

The 30 devotionals in this book discuss different aspects of faith—the faith necessary to know Christ, the faith that guides and comforts us in times of adversity and the faith we need to engage in spiritual battle. Here are some of the topics we cover:

- How faith enabled a couple to work through the pain of losing a son
- Why the Resurrection is the basis for our faith
- The importance of giving Christ authority in our lives
- How fear is the the opposite of faith
- The lies Satan uses to try to undermine our faith in God and His Word
- The trials that cause us to ask God, "Why?"
- Dealing with discouragement
- Sharing our faith with others

Throughout life we are all faced with situations in which we need to decide whether we believe God's Word or whether we believe our own feelings or thoughts. The more time we spend studying and applying God's Word, the stronger our faith in Him will grow. We challenge you to invest 15 minutes each day in your family by completing these devotionals with your spouse. You might consider reading them each night before you go to bed. And be sure to pray together afterward!

Note
1. Ney Bailey, *Faith Is Not a Feeling* (San Bernardino, CA: Here's Life Publishers, 1978), p. 24.

A CHRISTMAS I'LL NEVER FORGET

(PART ONE)

The LORD gave and the LORD has taken away.
Blessed be the name of the LORD.

JOB 1:21

*I*t was December 20, 1981. The kids were tucked in early, and Barbara and I were about to sit down for a nice quiet meal.

The phone rang and the voice at the other end had a chilling soberness to it that I shall never forget. I learned that my good friend Mick Yoder and two of his boys had been in a tragic plane crash that afternoon in Greenville, South Carolina.

Mick and his wife, Helen, had just moved to Greenville in the summer to start a church there. Only months before, Barbara and I had said good-bye to the Yoders after working with them for nearly five years to help start the ministry of FamilyLife.

That morning, Mick had preached and led the Sunday service at his church. Then he and his boys joined a couple for a plane ride. About two miles from the runway, a two-dollar part attached to the carburetor broke, and the plane lost all power. They missed the runway by only 10 feet and hit an embankment head-on.

Everyone survived the crash except for Mick's seven-year-old son, Benji. He died instantly.

The next morning, I kissed Barbara good-bye and flew to South Carolina. Nothing in all my years of ministry experience prepared me for what I beheld. Mick was in critical condition, with three of his four limbs broken. And Helen was numb from the emotional shock.

As I approached Mick's hospital bed, I was astounded at the number of tubes that made their way into his body. I leaned over his bed to attempt to comfort him by saying that hundreds around the country were praying and pulling for him and his family.

Mick nodded and then acknowledged the loss of Benji by quoting from Job 1:21: "The LORD gave and the LORD has taken away. Blessed be the name of the LORD."

And with those words, the sorrow that had left a lump in my throat caused my eyes to well up with tears.

Discuss: Discuss as a couple the kind of faith that it takes to make that kind of pronouncement that Mick did. Do you feel you are at the point where you could make the same expression of faith?

Pray: Ask God to help your faith grow. Pray that you will both become the man and the woman that God wants you to be.

A CHRISTMAS I'LL NEVER FORGET

(PART TWO)

*O death, where is your victory? O death,
where is your sting?*

1 CORINTHIANS 15:55

Mick was the only pastor for his small church in Greenville, so it fell upon me to conduct the graveside memorial services for Benji.

That day will forever be etched in my heart. There was a grayish-white coffin barely four feet long, holding the body of a seven-year-old boy. There was Benji's mom, Helen, with her 10-year-old son trying to stand strong and tall beside her. The rest of her family lay in a hospital, broken and nearly crushed. All of life seemed to have stopped and stood still.

What positive words could any man feebly utter in such a desperate moment? What could any man possibly have to say to a mother who would wake up on Christmas morning and look at the unopened presents for a boy she loved? Humanly, that moment was filled with injustice, questions, despair and anger. It was grim and dark.

But in the midst of the darkness of death, the star of Bethlehem suddenly shone bright. As I read from the Scriptures, the hope of the gospel of Jesus Christ came and swallowed up the darkness. "O death, where is your victory?"

I will never forget the contrast of agony and joy that day. If the gospel of Jesus Christ can bring hope and comfort to those who have just lost a child, then He is indeed all powerful. The tomb of Jesus Christ is empty. We can find forgiveness and peace with God because Christ is alive.

Many couples who lose a child, as Mick and Helen did, are never able to recover; and they end up divorcing. But somehow the Yoders were able to claim the victory that Christ promises. In fact, 14 months after Benji's death, Helen delivered a healthy baby girl. She and Mick named her Hope, as they claimed the promise of Jeremiah 29:11:

> "For I know the plans that I have for you," declares the LORD, "plans for welfare and not for calamity to give you a future and a hope."

Discuss: Do you believe God has your welfare in mind, no matter what happens to you?

Pray: Together pray that you will never lose hope in the midst of the challenges and tragedies of life.

IF THE GOSPEL OF JESUS
CHRIST CAN BRING HOPE AND
COMFORT TO THOSE WHO HAVE
JUST LOST A CHILD, THEN HE IS
INDEED ALL POWERFUL.

THE HINGE OF CHRISTIANITY

For if the dead are not raised, not even Christ has been raised; and if Christ has not been raised, your faith is worthless; you are still in your sins.

1 CORINTHIANS 15:16-17

I came across a fascinating list of questions that all have the same answer. Can you guess what it is?

- What gives a widow courage as she stands beside a fresh grave?

- What is the ultimate hope of the cripple, the amputee, the abused or the burn victim?

- How can parents of a brain-damaged or physically handicapped child keep from living their entire lives totally and completely depressed?

- Why would anyone who is blind or deaf or paralyzed be encouraged when he or she thinks of the life beyond?

- Where do the thoughts of a young couple go when they finally recover from the grief of losing their baby?

- When a family receives the tragic news that a little daughter was found dead or the dad was killed in a plane crash or the son overdosed on drugs, what single truth becomes their whole focus?
- What is the final answer to pain, mourning, senility, insanity, terminal diseases, sudden calamities and fatal accidents?

The answer to each of these questions is *the hope God gives us because of the bodily resurrection Jesus Christ offers to all who believe in Him.*

The reality is, Christianity hinges on the Resurrection. If Christ is not who He claimed to be and if He didn't come back from the dead, then as Paul said in 1 Corinthians 15:16-19, our "faith is worthless" and "we are of all men most to be pitied."

The pivotal point in all of human history is the resurrection of Christ. The one thing that separates Christianity from other religions is that God conquered death. And sin—my sin, your sin—was atoned for.

He is risen. Yes, Christ is risen indeed.

Discuss: How has the resurrection of Christ affected your life? What evidence can you give for the Resurrection?

Pray: Ask God to fill you with the hope of the Resurrection.

SEEING IS BELIEVING

*Jesus said to [Thomas], "Because you have
seen Me, have you believed? Blessed are they
who did not see, and yet believed."*

JOHN 20:29

Have you ever noticed how some businesses creatively communicate a service or product through a catchy name or slogan? Recently the name of a Christian optometrist's practice grabbed my attention: "Seeing Is Believing." When I saw that, my mind raced back to the year I graduated from junior college.

I was a normal 20-year-old in the midst of the tumultuous '60s. Although everything I had touched during the previous year had turned to gold—grades, girls and college athletics—my life was chock-full of compromise, doubt, perplexing questions I couldn't answer and frequent despair. Among my many questions were, Is the Bible really God's Word? Why does God allow suffering? If Christianity is a hoax, what is the purpose of life?

Precariously balanced with one foot on the banana peel of doubt and the other foot in the world, I began to honestly seek what God had to say about my life. Throughout my quest one question haunted me: Must I really see it to believe it? You see, my life really was riddled with questions I couldn't answer. But in the fall of 1968, God loved me out of my unbelief. He helped me realize that I needed to look at the answers I couldn't escape.

I knew the Resurrection was true. If Christ were still in the tomb, then Christianity had little more to offer me than other world religions. But it is an irrefutable fact of history—Christ is risen.

I knew the Bible to be true. We have more evidence of the historical authenticity of today's Bible than we have of any other historical document of comparable age.

Science and archaeology continue to prove (rather than disprove) the Bible's historical accuracy. And the Bible's central theme remains clear: God loves humankind and wants to redeem men and women to Himself. The Bible also tells us how to live. It gives us hope in the face of death. And it contains the best set of blueprints for building a home (a marriage and family) that I've ever seen.

One additional truth helped erase my doubts: I knew that the risen Lord Jesus Christ lived in me. He came to change my life. As I focused on the facts of Christianity, I began to see the scales of faith tip toward belief. I began to base my life on what I knew to be true.

What have been the results?

- A life that is an adventure—walking with God is electrifying
- A lasting sense of destiny and significance that

isn't man-made or fake
- The privilege of being used by God for eternal purposes
- His Holy Spirit's empowerment to deny my selfishness and to love people
- A sense of peace, well-being and contentment that can only come when I obey Him

The phrase "seeing is believing" may work for a Christian optometrist, but if you wait to believe until you have answers for all your doubts and questions, you'll be waiting until it's too late!

Discuss: What are the questions about God or Christianity that have caused you to doubt God's existence? Be honest with your spouse about your questions.

Pray: Ask God to give you an inner conviction of the truth of Scripture, or the answers you cannot escape. If you've never done so, give God total control of your life right now. And if you've already done that but have since taken back ownership, you need to reestablish who is going to be Lord of your life.

GOD LOVED ME OUT OF MY UNBELIEF.

THE AUTHORITY OF CHRIST

(PART ONE)

And Jesus said to them, "Follow Me, and I will make you become fishers of men."

MARK 1:17

*I*n Mark we find Christ meeting Simon and Andrew as they were casting fishing nets into the sea. He challenges them to follow Him, and they spend a couple of weeks making their decisions—calculating whether following Christ would cost them financially, determining if it would damage their reputations.

Wrong. Simon and Andrew *immediately* left the nets and followed Him. They instantly recognized Christ's authority in their lives.

I believe that one of the reasons why we don't see more people leaving their nets and following Christ is because we in the Church have not presented the authentic, real, living Lord Jesus in all of His splendor, majesty and glory. When we see Him for who He is, no possession, no worldly honor, no earthly success can compare with the King of kings.

Not all who see Jesus continue following Him. John 6 records that after Christ made some difficult and challenging statements, "Many of His disciples withdrew, and were not walking with Him anymore" (v. 66). Then Jesus asked the remaining 12, "You do not want to go away also, do you?" (v. 67).

And Peter made a profound statement: "Lord, to whom shall we go? You have words of eternal life" (v. 68). He had come to the conclusion that there was no other to follow.

The longer I am in the Christian life, the more I see that nothing matters other than Jesus Christ and His Word. In recent days I've asked Him to infuse my life with the conviction that He alone is worth following.

Discuss: Do you know of someone who has withdrawn and no longer follows Jesus? How has that decision affected his or her life and the lives of those near them? Have you left your nets to follow Jesus?

Pray: Pray that you will grow in your hunger and thirst for knowing the One who has the words of eternal life.

DAY 6

THE AUTHORITY OF CHRIST

(PART TWO)

The Spirit of the Lord is upon Me, because He anointed
Me to preach the gospel to the poor. He has sent Me to
proclaim release to the captives, and recovery of sight
to the blind, to set free those who are downtrodden,
to proclaim the favorable year of the Lord.

LUKE 4:18-19

When we give Christ authority in our lives, we discover that He has the ability to make our lives so much better than they would be without Him. Just look at the verses from Luke, for example.

Are you brokenhearted over a child or over a relationship with a family member or some other person? These heartbreaks and sorrows are a part of life. I have faced too many of them and found myself without any word for them. But Jesus said to give Him our hurts and sorrows.

Will you take your broken heart with you to the grave and end up hopeless? Or will you take your broken heart to Christ and let the Great Physician heal you on His authority?

Jesus said He can heal the brokenhearted.

In addition, Jesus has authority over sin. Nothing gives us freedom and heals our sorrows more than forgiveness of sins. Look at Mark 2:5, which records Jesus' words to the paralytic: "My son, your sins are forgiven." And then, to squash grumbling among the scribes who said only God has such authority, He proved who He was by healing the same man (see vv. 6-12)!

Finally, He has authority over death. We see this in the raising of Lazarus in John 11 and then, of course, through His own resurrection.

Knowing you have eternal life because of Christ gives new meaning and hope to your years on Earth. As Jesus said, "O death, where is your victory?" (1 Cor. 15:55).

Discuss: What is causing heartbreak and sorrow in your life right now? Have you spent time talking with God about it?

Pray: Ask God to give you hope and joy in the midst of troubled times.

WILL YOU TAKE YOUR
BROKEN HEART TO CHRIST
AND LET THE GREAT
PHYSICIAN HEAL YOU?

BEHOLD HIS GLORY

In My Father's house are many dwelling places . . .
for I go to prepare a place for you.

JOHN 14:2

One of the greatest ways to learn about God is to spend some time looking at His creation. His power, His majesty, His beauty and His incredible creativity are evident in the world He made.

But that's not all you'll learn. I'll never forget going up on a ski lift with a friend on a frosty February morning. On our left was a range of 13,000-foot peaks. To our right was a beautiful lake surrounded by a host of mountains.

I shook my head and said, "Isn't it amazing to see what God made?" And my friend replied, "Yeah, and God made this in a day. And 2,000 years ago Christ said He would be preparing a place for us. And He's been gone 2,000 years preparing that place for us. Heaven is going to be a magnificent place!"

As a child I used to think heaven would be boring. What would I do for all eternity—sit around and strum a harp? But my friend's statement helped me realize that although I have no idea what heaven will be like, it will be much, much, much greater than I can even imagine.

Why is it that we resist moving into this our heavenly home? If you went to the doctor this afternoon and learned you had an incurable form of cancer, you wouldn't initially be smiling. You would be depressed, fearful and worried about your family and loved ones.

But we're all going to die eventually, and I think God has given us a beautiful world so that we can behold just a glimpse of what is in store for us. I love what one person said: "Nature is God's Braille for a blind humanity." Nature is God's way to help us see Him even though we don't have the eyes to really behold His glory.

Discuss: Take a walk in the woods or in the country and take some time to behold God's creation. What do you learn about His character—and about heaven—from what you see?

Pray: Take an after-dinner drive to a beautiful park or overlook. Worship the God of all creation, who died for you!

A BASEMENT FULL OF FEARS

There is no fear in love; but perfect love casts out fear.

1 JOHN 4:18

I don't remember when my brother told me about "the creature," but I can recall as a little tyke standing at the top of the stairs looking down into the deep darkness of our basement. It was a dark, damp and dingy kind of place. Of course, I didn't know it, but my brother pulled a trick on me when he told me about the grisliest, meanest bogeyman you've ever seen.

On occasion, my mom would send me downstairs to get some canned green beans or some potatoes she stored in our basement. You've never seen a kid run so fast. I'd set a world record going down and up those stairs. Although I never saw that bogeyman, I heard him frequently. And it scared the daylights out of me. In fact, to this day when I stand at the top of those same stairs, I still feel a leftover trace of that same fear.

Are there any bogeymen in your life? You may couch it in terms like "I'm concerned about this" or "I've been thinking about this a lot." But any way you slice it, most of us are fearful. We're fearful about the future, about where our lives our going. We're even fearful of God's will.

Hate is not the opposite of love; fear is. As 1 John 4:18 says, "Perfect love casts out fear." To be secure in God's love and protection of us, we must have faith. And we can't manufacture such spiritual fruit ourselves. Sheer effort alone does not make good fruit grow. Zechariah 4:6 says, "'Not by might nor by power, but by My Spirit,' says the LORD of hosts." As God's Spirit works in us and through us to develop this fruit, He will take away our fears and fill us with His love.

Discuss: What are your top three fears in life right now? Share them with one another, and talk about why you are afraid in each of these areas.

Pray: Pray for you and your spouse to be delivered from all your fears, and ask God to begin filling both of you with His love and with His Spirit.

HATE IS NOT THE OPPOSITE
OF LOVE; FEAR IS.

THE TOP-FIVE
FEAR LIST

The fear of man brings a snare, but he who
trusts in the LORD will be exalted.

PROVERBS 29:25

A college professor did a survey of 2,000 students and asked them what their greatest fears were. Here is the list of their top five fears:

1. Public speaking
2. Blindness
3. Heights
4. Heart attack or cancer
5. Death

Fear is a snare, a trap. It paralyzes and discourages us. It intimidates us and causes us to feel inferior to others and to our circumstances. I believe fear operates like a magnifying glass, making seemingly small objects and circumstances seem giant and insurmountable.

Today, I believe too many Christians suffer from what I call the What-If Syndrome. Like a dog chasing its tail, each of those What-If Christians doesn't make any decisions because of the continual worry "What if . . . ?" This is exactly how the devil wants us to think.

You see, if Satan can get fear to line the interior of our soul, it becomes like an impenetrable coating that causes us to take our focus off God. Satan will do all he can to keep us from yielding our lives to God and experiencing His peace and love. First Peter 5:8 tells us, "Be of sober spirit, be on the alert. Your adversary, the devil, prowls about like a roaring lion, seeking someone to devour." He is trying to use the snare of fear to devour us!

But God's Word says, "He who trusts in the LORD will be exalted" (Prov. 29:25). And although Satan may win a few battles on this earth, the victory is God's in the end.

Fear is the emotional pain in the soul of unbelief. When we feel fearful, it is God's warning light to us that we need to respond with faith; fear and faith cannot exist simultaneously in our souls.

Discuss: Look at the list of fears you wrote yesterday. How are those fears causing you to take your focus off God?

Pray: Pray that God would fill your heart with faith so that you will have the ability to trust Him in fearful circumstances.

SATAN'S LIES TO FAMILIES

(PART ONE)

*[The devil] was a murderer from the beginning, and does
not stand in the truth, because there is no truth in him.*

JOHN 8:44

The Desert Storm conflict that Saddam Hussein fueled in
1990-1991 caused me to reflect on the spiritual battle that
daily swirls around your family and ours.

Families don't seem to talk about spiritual battles
much. Our enemy is unseen. The theater for operations and
battles—our souls (our minds, emotions and wills)—does
not appear on any map. Maybe it sounds a little too mysti-
cal for us to think of life as being more than what is seen,
but the Bible says spiritual battles are real. And what is at
stake is of the utmost importance.

Joe Louis, one of the greatest heavyweight boxers of all
time, was once asked about the secret of his success. Louis
responded by saying that he and his manager always stud-
ied each opponent thoroughly. As a result, Louis said, he
was seldom *surprised* and was able to stay on the *offensive*
throughout the entire fight.

I feel that too many Christians are uninformed about Satan and his tactics. As a result, many are living defensive, shell-shocked lifestyles. I want to help you stay on the offensive and win your family's encounters with the adversary by learning one of his primary strategies.

A good friend, Ney Bailey, made a profound statement about our spiritual adversary, Satan, and his daily tactics on our spiritual lives: *"The only power that Satan has is in his lies and getting us to believe them."*

It was interesting to watch how Saddam Hussein used lies to intimidate, create fear and keep us off balance in battle. During the first 24 hours of the ground-war offensive, Baghdad radio reported, "Allied troops are dying like flies." I felt afraid. I just knew he had killed thousands of our troops with chemical and biological weapons. I felt that perhaps this ground war was not such a good idea after all; maybe we should pull out and go home.

But I was believing a lie. It was only as the truth became clear that my fears were relieved: Our forces were achieving overwhelming victory.

Satan knows better than Saddam Hussein that his real power in your life is through his lies.

Discuss: How frequently do you doubt God's Word? What lies undermine your faith in God and His Word?

Pray: In prayer, resist the devil—the promise is he will flee from you (see Jas. 4:7). Ask God to help you recognize your real enemy, spot the lies and grow in faith.

SATAN KNOWS WELL THAT
HIS REAL POWER IN YOUR LIFE
IS THROUGH HIS LIES.

SATAN'S LIES TO FAMILIES

(PART TWO)

Whenever [the devil] speaks a lie, he speaks from his own nature; for he is a liar, and the father of lies.

JOHN 8:44

I can think of at least four lies Satan tells families:

1. "You're a failure. You'll never make it." The lie of self-condemnation is one of Satan's chief weapons. You may struggle with feelings of guilt, failure or inferiority. Satan would have you believe that your faults are much too damaging to be covered by the grace of God. If you believe this lie, it renders you powerless, passive and paralyzed, without any hope of progress as parents.

2. "You don't deserve to be unhappy." Of course God does want you to be happy, but the way Satan puts the statement is a lie because he means, "All you need to do is get out from under this relationship or these family pressures and you'll be happy." It's

a "feel-good lie" because what really feels good is working through problems together.

3. "Nobody will find out." Have you ever heard a little voice tempting you to do something illegal or immoral that would bring instant satisfaction or pleasure? You may think nobody will discover what you do, but that's a lie. The truth will come out.

4. "If I had what Sam has, I'd be happier." Satan wants you to think that what you have is inferior to what someone else has. The lie is exposed when you realize that such comparisons are always made from a distance. If you had what Sam had, you would probably experience Sam-type problems, and they may be worse than yours.

Remember that Satan is a counterfeiter. If you refuse to believe his lies, he is rendered powerless. Resist him by remembering the truth of God's Word.

Discuss: Which of these lies do you see Satan using with you? Be specific.

Pray: Pray that a sense of God's own power will fill your heart and that His voice through the Word will drown out each of Satan's lies.

Discoveries from Difficulties

And the rain descended, and the floods came, and the winds blew, and burst against that house; and yet it did not fall, for it had been founded upon the rock.

MATTHEW 7:25

I see two major ways in which families fail to respond properly to adversity. First, and most typically, *they fail to anticipate the trials and problems that will come.* When Jesus spoke of building our lives on a sure foundation, He seemed to *assume* that the rains would come and the winds would blow.

To the well-known saying that only death and taxes are certain, we can add that troubles are certain, too. And a joke I read says, "The man whose problems are all behind him is probably a school bus driver."

Second, when troubles do hit, *many couples simply don't know how to respond.* They have no foundation in Christ, no plan for dealing with the pain—so they turn against one another.

I was just ending a FamilyLife Conference in Dallas when a trim, muscular gentleman came up to greet me. He was a

Green Beret. I had touched a nerve with him when I talked about the need to have a plan for facing problems. He told me: "Dennis, in the Green Berets we train over and over, and then over and over again. We repeat some exercises until we are sick of them, but our instructors know what they are doing. They want us so prepared and finely trained that when trials and difficulties come on the battlefield, we will be able to fall back upon that which has become second nature to us. We literally learn to respond by reflex action."

Families—especially parents—should be so well grounded in God's plan that their reaction to a crisis or difficulty will be an automatic reflex, not a panic. If you wait until a crisis hits and then turn to the Scriptures, you won't be as prepared—and you'll be more vulnerable to the enemy.

Discuss: If a life-altering crisis were to hit your family tomorrow, do you feel you'd be ready?

Pray: Ask God to enable you, when crises strike, to call on your long-standing faith in Christ and the life of trust you have built on Him.

FAMILIES SHOULD BE SO
WELL GROUNDED IN GOD'S
PLAN THAT THEIR REACTION
TO A CRISIS WILL BE AN
AUTOMATIC REFLEX.

THE BEST AND WORST OF TIMES

(PART ONE)

And not only this, but we also exult in our tribulations, knowing that tribulation brings about perseverance; and perseverance, proven character; and proven character, hope.

ROMANS 5:3-4

To begin his classic novel *A Tale of Two Cities*, Charles Dickens penned the immortal words: "It was the best of times, it was the worst of times." Was Dickens indulging in an overstated contradiction? Hardly. Life is both sweet and sour—simultaneously. As Louis Adamic, author of *The Native's Return*, is known to have said, "Life is like licking honey off a thorn."

Some time ago I was tasting the sweet savor of a great year. It was the best of times in that our FamilyLife Conferences were growing rapidly. At the same time, I was stretched thin by the adversary: pressure, attacks, seemingly insurmountable problems—the worst of times.

Then, as Barbara and I were beginning to get our strength back, we learned she was pregnant—again—and it was not planned, at least not by us. It would mean that in God's sovereign and loving will, we'd have six children aged 10 and under. The best of times?

Then came that day when God really got our attention. Barbara walked into our bedroom and fell on the bed, complaining that her heart was beating too fast. As we sped to the hospital, a hundred thoughts flashed through my mind. Praying for Barbara, I wondered how quickly the doctors would be able to slow her heart. Would I soon be saying good-bye to the woman I loved and be left alone to raise five children?

Were these the worst of times? *No!* Not for a Christian. For even death—the selfish, cursed enemy of man—has been "swallowed up in victory" (1 Cor. 15:54). Even tribulations, the Scriptures tell us, produce hope (see Rom. 5:3-4).

But I don't like this way of producing hope, I thought as our van rounded the corner to the hospital. *We don't need this right now.*

Fascinating, isn't it, how quickly our lives can be reduced to a simple faith in God. I've wondered on more than one occasion if God doesn't shake His head at how slow we are to realize we are not in control!

Discuss: Have you been through some "worst of times" in which your faith grew? What situations seem to test your faith the most? Why?

Pray: Ask God to strengthen your faith so that in good times or bad proven character will result.

THE BEST AND WORST OF TIMES

(PART TWO)

The conclusion, when all has been heard, is:
fear God and keep His commandments.

ECCLESIASTES 12:13

The doctors went to work on Barbara while Christians across the country prayed. Her heart beat so quickly (200 to 300 beats per minute) that it was not filling with blood, and her blood pressure went down. This blood low pressure could harm the baby if it continued.

The doctor made a quick decision. Using electric shock, he successfully reduced Barbara's heart rate to 75 beats per minute. Afterward, through tears, we gave thanks for God's intervention in saving both Barbara and the baby.

We talked quite a bit after that terrifying event. Often we *think* we are in control. We think we can plan our lives. We struggle with so many insignificant things that we eventually find ourselves asking, *What really matters?*

In the midst of these best and worst of times, a certain book in the Bible reached us like a beacon in the darkness.

It's a book that rips away the veil of idealism about life. It deals with purpose and significance. It gives meaning to life's storms, to prosperity, to our search for security.

The book? Ecclesiastes.

In its pages Solomon paints the paradoxes of life better than Charles Dickens ever dreamed of. Whether we're experiencing the best or worst of times, God must be our reference point (see Eccles. 12:13). If not, then life is empty—void of meaning.

As I drove away from the hospital later that afternoon, I reflected on how different people respond to crisis situations. And I wondered, *What is their reference point for a life-and-death situation? Where do they find meaning? How do they make sense out of suffering?*

That night, as I put our five children to bed, we crowded together and prayed. Benjamin, then eight, prayed as only a child can: "Father, we give thanks that Mommy got sick 'cause we know You want us to give thanks in everything . . . and we give thanks that she's okay, too."

He prayed with childlike faith and a mature perspective. He understood how God wants us to respond in the best *and* worst of times. Sometimes it takes a child's faith in God to remind us, doesn't it?

Discuss: For what tribulations can you thank God today?

Pray: Pray that you would learn to fear God and that He would be your reference point in the best and worst of times.

SOMETIMES IT TAKES A
CHILD'S FAITH TO REMIND US
OF HOW GOD WANTS US TO
RESPOND IN THE BEST *AND*
WORST OF TIMES.

DIVINE SUFFICIENCY

And such confidence we have through Christ toward God.
Not that we are adequate in ourselves to consider anything
as coming from ourselves, but our adequacy is from God.

2 CORINTHIANS 3:4-5

*I*t's so easy to feel overwhelmed by life. When you consider your responsibilities in marriage, family, work, church and extended family, feelings of inadequacy and hopelessness can rise suddenly and envelop you like a thick fog.

Yet you can keep from being overwhelmed by focusing on the sufficiency of Christ. He is alive today, and He stands ready to guide you along the way. Nancy Spiegelberg's poem "If Only I Had Known You" beautifully expresses these truths:

> Lord, I crawled across the barrenness to You with
>   my empty cup
> Uncertain in asking any small drop of refreshment.
> If only I had known You better
> I'd have come running with a bucket.[1]

God wants you to know Him, to receive His blessings and to live a life of peace, purpose and pardon. The Bible contains many wonderful principles and truths, but these principles will be only stale dogma and doctrine to you unless you allow the person of Jesus Christ to be at the center of your life. As A. W. Tozer states, "What comes into our minds when we think about God is the most important thing about us."[2]

No matter how inadequate you feel to fulfill your responsibilities, God is completely able to do what appears impossible. His power is most evident when you are at your weakest. As Paul says in Philippians 4:13, "I can do all things through Him who strengthens me."

Why not submit to Him today and ask Him to be your sufficiency and your strength?

Discuss: In what areas do you feel inadequate? How has God proven His sufficiency to you in the past?

Pray: Ask God to help you trust in His sufficiency even when you feel you are unable to do anything worthy on your own.

Notes

1. © 1981 Nancy Spiegelberg. Reprinted by permission of the author.
2. A. W. Tozer, *The Knowledge of the Holy* (San Francisco: Harper, 1998), p.1.

TRUST IN A SOVEREIGN GOD

On the contrary, who are you, O man, who answers
back to God? The thing molded will not say to the molder,
"Why did you make me like this," will it?

ROMANS 9:20

I once heard a pastor say that on any given day, 90 percent of the families in his congregation are facing some challenge or crisis. Such a crisis struck our own family when our son Samuel at the age of 16 was diagnosed with muscular dystrophy.

Let me confess that I've come close to talking back to God over this and many other issues. After more than 30 years of trying to yield to Christ's rule, experiences of my own and others often leave me with several thorny questions that remain unanswered:

- Why would God allow some children to be sexually molested?
- Why do so many couples who want children find themselves infertile?

- Why do some spouses who have every reason to remain faithful suddenly abandon their families?

I don't believe Scripture provides simple answers to these questions. But I do believe that Romans 9:20 gives a strong overall answer that invites me to embrace the deepest hope and the strongest faith.

When the Bible asserts that God, the divine Potter, is in control, it raises for some the question of why He allows this or that to happen. But it also invites supreme confidence that however tragic its effects, evil does not have the last word. A loving God who has sovereign control over the world can also be trusted to overwhelm present evils.

In our own family's situation, a hint of how God's power can enable us to overcome tragedy came one evening when Samuel and I were driving home from the grocery store. We had been talking about his limitations due to MD. Samuel turned from gazing out the window, looked at me and said resolutely, "Well, Dad, I guess you don't need legs to serve God."

Discuss: For what situations are you asking God, "Why?" Has He given you a reply?

Pray: Ask God to give you the ability to trust Him in any situation.

A LOVING GOD WHO
HAS SOVEREIGN CONTROL
OVER THE WORLD CAN ALSO
BE TRUSTED TO OVERWHELM
PRESENT EVILS.

PEBBLES IN MY SHOES

*Rejoice always; pray without ceasing; in everything give
thanks; for this is God's will for you in Christ Jesus.*

1 THESSALONIANS 5:16-18

$\mathcal{D}$o you ever feel as though the "little" circumstances of life
are about to overwhelm you? As the Canadian poet Robert
Service said, "It isn't the mountain ahead that wears you
out—it's the grain of sand in your shoe." I agree.

Would you like to know what pebbles seem to frequent
my sneakers?

- People who try to make me feel guilty
- My unbalanced checkbook
- The incessant ringing of the telephone
- Sibling rivalry
- A drippy faucet, a smoky fireplace, a leaky pipe in
  the ceiling
- A whining child
- An unresolved conflict with a family member
- More sibling rivalry

For many years I didn't react well to those nagging little
problems. I was used to calling things bad luck, getting ticked

off or just shrugging my shoulders while muttering "What's the use?" Then I discovered 1 Thessalonians 5:18, and I began to measure my walk with God by these four simple words: "In everything give thanks." To my amazement, I started to notice a change in my attitude about life in general. I began to realize that God wants to pervade every area of my life.

Let me suggest three reasons God commanded us to give thanks in all things. First, *giving thanks in all things expresses faith*—faith in the God who knows what He's doing, faith in the God who sovereignly rules in all that happens to us. Isn't that what He wants from us?

Second, *He knew we wouldn't do it naturally.* Giving thanks in all things means we no longer walk as a mere human, grumbling and griping, but walk as a spiritual human (see 1 Cor. 2:14-15)—a human who sees God at work, even in the pebbles that tend to fill our shoes.

Finally, God wants to teach us how to deal with the irritating pebbles *so that we can get on with climbing the mountains He has for us.* All we see are the pebbles, and we think if we could just remove all those pebbles, then we could get on with real life. But the pebbles are the real life that God brings us day by day. He wants to use those irritants to instruct us and to see us mature in Christ.

Discuss: Do you have some pebbles in your shoe that feel like a herd of boulders? What are those irritants?

Pray: Before you try to empty your shoes, why don't you stop right now and give thanks for that rock pile. Tell God you want to submit to Him to learn the lessons He has for you in the midst of daily life, and ask Him to teach you through these pebbles that are in your shoes.

DEALING WITH DISCOURAGEMENT

*And let us not lose heart in doing good, for in due time
we shall reap if we do not grow weary.*

GALATIANS 6:9

A story is told about a public auction that the devil held.
As the prospective buyers assembled, they noticed Satan was
selling his tools of worry, fear, lust, greed and selfishness.
But off to one side, standing alone, was one well-worn tool
labeled "Not for sale."

Asked to explain, the devil replied, "I can spare my other
tools, but I cannot spare this one. It is the most useful implement that I have. It is called Discouragement, and with it I
can work my way deep into hearts otherwise inaccessible."

What tools do you need to overcome discouragement?
First, *be truthful*. I've found that God is not fooled by my lofty
prayers for the missionaries in Africa, when deep inside I'm
hurting. God is able to handle your emotions. Be honest
with yourself and God about your disappointment.

Second, *pray about it*. Are you discouraged about a child
who rarely reaches your expectations? Tell God. Disheartened

about your mate and an unresolved conflict? God knows already, but pour it out.

Third, *find the source of your discouragement*. Sometimes it's a goal that was not attained—again. Or the problem may be a friend's cutting remark, the feeling that you're carrying a particularly heavy burden alone or the lack of approval by an important person in your life.

By isolating the source of my discouragement, I have often found that my hope has been in the wrong person or in the wrong place. Or I've found that my response has been normal—and because I can't quit, I've just got to work through my feelings of wanting to throw in the towel.

Fourth, with a heart of faith *look beyond your circumstances and your emotions* to a God who will renew you day by day. Realize that God uses hardship to perfect your faith (see Rom. 5:1-10). God promises that you'll one day reap if you don't grow weary.

Discuss: What is causing you discouragement right now? Which of the tools do you need to use to combat discouragement?

Pray: Get on your knees and pray that neither of you would grow weary and lose heart.

GOD USES HARDSHIP TO PERFECT YOUR FAITH.

PARENTAL DISCOURAGEMENT

BY BARBARA RAINEY

*In this you greatly rejoice, . . . that the proof of your faith,
being more precious than gold, . . . even though tested
by fire, may be found to result in praise and glory and
honor at the revelation of Jesus Christ.*

1 PETER 1:6-7

$\mathcal{D}$o you want to know the chief emotion mothers feel today?
It's not anger, worry, fear, loneliness or lack of confidence. It's
discouragement. It begins as exasperation and can easily
become a feeling of being out of control.

At times raising six kids has a way of getting us discouraged. I remember our going once to a pancake house
and the kids were really at each other's throats. Dennis and
I were thinking, *We're failures. We're raising juvenile delinquents.
Here we are speaking at conferences and on the radio every day, and
we're failures!*

But that is just part of raising kids. If there is anyone
who is doing it perfectly, then he or she had better peel back
the cover on their kid and find out if he or she is a robot. We

don't raise robots; we raise kids with wills of their own. They are going to disappoint us and we will be discouraged.

I think Christians are more susceptible to discouragement because our standard is holiness—nothing less than 100 percent perfection. Somehow we start believing that our faith will eliminate failure. In reality, our faith will help us battle the discouragement that comes after failure.

We need to hold on to our faith. "Being more precious than gold," our faith combined with a lot of perseverance will result in an imperishable reward—and a generation of children who are raised up in Him.

Discuss: How does discouragement and raising a family impact you? How can you come alongside your spouse to encourage and support one another?

Pray: Ask the Lord to help you and your mate allow yourselves the freedom to fail as parents, and to teach you how to handle those times when you feel like failures.

DEADWOOD

*Blessed is a man who perseveres under trial; for once he
has been approved, he will receive the crown of life.*

JAMES 1:12

*L*loyd Shadrach, a pastor in Franklin, Tennessee, once told
me about walking down a road after a thunderstorm and
stepping over dead limbs that the wind had blown off a row
of mature trees. "It was as though God was giving me a per-
sonal object lesson of what storms can do in our lives," he
said.

"In the middle of the storm when the wind is gusting,
the lightning is popping and the storm clouds are getting
darker, it's difficult to believe that our troubles are purpose-
ful. But God may allow a storm in our lives to clear out the
deadwood so that new growth can occur. And isn't it interesting how fresh the air feels after a storm is over?"

As Lloyd shared his parable with me, I couldn't help but
reflect on the deadwood, several cords of it, that storms have
blown from my life over the years. One of the most important things Barbara and I have learned from these storms is
that God is interested in our growth. He wants us to trust
Him in the midst of the storms, grow together as a couple

and not fall apart. The storms of life enable family members to depend on each other and discover new strength in God.

Discuss: How have you reacted to the storms in your life? Have they drawn you closer as a couple, or have you allowed them to drive you apart?

Pray: Ask God to enable your family to persevere in all trials. Pray about a specific problem, asking God to use it to help your family discover strength in Jesus Christ.

GOD WANTS US TO
TRUST HIM IN THE MIDST
OF THE STORMS.

ENTERING LION COUNTRY

We know that we are of God, and the whole
world lies in the power of the evil one.

1 JOHN 5:19

*I*nstead of falling prey to the devil, Christians must be aggressive soldiers who seek to recapture the land for Christ. One goal of our spiritual battle is to prevent our adversary from having any sphere of influence in our lives.

Successful invaders are risk takers, men and women of faith and action. The victory will go to those who move their faith the 18-inch distance from their heads to their hearts. Many Christians, however, seem to prefer comfort to conflict.

I believe the great issues of our day will only be decided when well-equipped Christians invade lion country—territory controlled by the devil (see 1 Pet. 5:8). C. T. Studd, a missionary to China, understood this challenge well. He wrote, "Some want to live within the sound of church or chapel bell; I want to run a rescue shop within a yard of hell."

As you encroach on the enemy's territory, remember these admonitions from Scripture:

- Stand firm, and let God's Word be your guide. You have God's assurance that you won't lose the war (see Eph. 6:14-17).
- Pray always, and give thanks (see 1 Thess. 5:17-18).
- Don't take temptation lightly; flee immorality (see 2 Tim. 2:22).
- Walk by faith, not by what you feel and see. God's Word and His promises are either 100 percent true or they are not true at all. Since His Word is true, your faith is the difference. Grab hold of His Word, and step out (see 2 Cor. 5:7).

The battle has been tough recently, but I wouldn't trade being in lion country for any of the peace and comfort that depend on compromise. What about you?

Discuss: Talk with your mate about enemy territory you want to reclaim as a couple.

Pray: Spend some time in prayer asking God to show you the enemy territory He wants you to invade. Ask Him for wisdom, guidance and power to stand firm in the battle.

RUNNING TO WIN

*And everyone who competes in the games exercises
self-control in all things. They then do it to receive a
perishable wreath, but we an imperishable. Therefore I run
in such a way, as not without aim; I box in such a way,
as not beating the air; but I buffet my body and make
it my slave, lest possibly, after I have preached to others,
I myself should be disqualified.*

1 CORINTHIANS 9:25-27

If you're running in the race of the Christian life, don't let anyone hinder you from running well. But has it ever occurred to you that you could be disqualified in the race? We toy with disqualification when we repeatedly reject God's leading in our lives—this is an act of willful, deliberate disobedience.

Look around at the human debris of those who have been disqualified from usefulness to God. I don't condemn those who fail—I stand in ministry today because of the grace of God in my life. But those who have been disqualified have become examples warning me that I, too, could be disqualified and declared no longer usable by God.

How do you run to win? Here are Paul's rules for the race:

1. *Exercise self-control in all things.* The discipline of our desires is the backbone of character. Know what tempts you, and avoid it. Augustine, the great Christian philosopher, lived a licentious life before his conversion. One day, shortly after becoming a believer, Augustine encountered a young woman with whom he had sinned. Augustine turned immediately and began running away as the woman cried out, "Augustine! Augustine! It is I! It is I!" But Augustine just kept running and yelled back over his shoulder, "It isn't I! It isn't I! It isn't I!"

2. *Know where you are going.* The finish line for the Christian is standing face-to-face with the Person of Jesus Christ in eternity. Keep your eyes on Him. Grow in your love for Him. Be pleasing to Him.

3. *Be willing to sacrifice.* The Christian life will cost you your life. You and I must deny our rights and die to ourselves.

Run to win. It's the only race that really counts!

Discuss: Is there anything in your life right now that could disqualify you? Share with your spouse any temptations you may be facing.

Pray: Pray that you and your spouse will withstand temptations and lead holy lives.

THE FINISH LINE FOR
THE CHRISTIAN IS STANDING
FACE-TO-FACE WITH THE
PERSON OF JESUS CHRIST
IN ETERNITY.

THE FEAR OF FAILURE

Love covers a multitude of sins.

1 PETER 4:8

*I*n an address to a nation divided by the Civil War, Abraham Lincoln underscored the need to persevere in spite of failure. He said, "I am not concerned that you have fallen—I am concerned that you arise." The following excerpt, which appeared in an advertisement in the *Wall Street Journal,* also emphasizes this point:

> You've failed many times although you may not remember. You fell the first time you tried to walk, didn't you? You almost drowned the first time you tried to swim. Did you hit the ball the first time you swung the bat? Heavy hitters, the ones who hit the most home runs, also struck out a lot. R. H. Macy failed seven times before his store in New York caught on. English novelist John Cracey got 753 rejection slips before he published 564 books. Babe Ruth struck out 1330 times, but he also hit 714 home runs. Don't worry about failure. Worry about the chances you miss when you don't even try.

In a performance-oriented culture such as ours, failure belts us like a punch in the stomach. Repeated failure often results in a knockout blow, and many of us give up altogether. As Comedian W. C. Fields once quipped, "If at first you don't succeed, then quit. There's no use in being a fool about it."

The problem is that a life with little failure is a life of little risk. This type of life may appear to offer safety and security, but it actually leads to guilt, boredom, further apathy and even lower self-esteem. God designed and commissioned us to be productive—many times that demands faith and risk.

Do you and your mate have the freedom to fail? Are you assured of each other's love—no matter what mistakes you make? By slowly forging in each other the freedom to fail, you'll become more open to change, more willing to take risks and more confident in decision making.

Discuss: Evaluate your own fear of failure. Are you a risk taker? Are decisions difficult? How would you evaluate your mate? What can you do to encourage him or her to move past fears?

Pray: Ask God to give you enough faith to move beyond your fears and trust Him, even in the midst of failure.

THE EASIEST THING TO DO IS NOTHING

Let us not lose heart in doing good.

GALATIANS 6:9

*I*t's no secret that America is in the midst of a spiritual and moral crisis. Polls today indicate that most Americans are deeply concerned about the direction our nation is heading. The real problem is a critical shortage of people who care enough to get off the sidelines and make a difference. Sometimes it only takes one person to turn the flow from negative to positive.

Take, for instance, Babe Ruth, the most famous baseball player of all time. Babe finished his career in a slump, and according to one legendary story, he was jeered mercilessly one day in Cincinnati. As he made his customary trot off the field to the dugout, the fans began to yell obscenities at him. The booing intensified until a little boy jumped a fence and ran to his hero's side.

The child threw his arms around Babe's legs, crying as he fiercely hugged him. Moved by the young lad's display of affection and emotion, Babe gently swept the boy upwards and into his arms. As Babe walked off the field carrying the boy, the man and boy cried together.

Suddenly, the hoots, howls and curses ceased. And the eerie silence was replaced by a thunderous ovation. Fans of all ages now began to weep. One small boy's courageous actions had changed the behavior of thousands of people.

I can't help but wonder how long the boy sat there listening to the cursing, angry crowd before he did something. Probably not very long.

And today, how much worse must our nation become before individuals are moved by compassion and conviction to get out of their seats and make a difference?

As I pray for our nation and its families, I continue to sense that the battle will be won by lay men and women like you. As Paul exhorted in Galatians 6:9, "Let us not lose heart in doing good."

Discuss: In what ways are you concerned about the direction our country is headed?

Pray: Ask God to burden your heart with the need to be involved in the battle.

LET US NOT LOSE HEART IN DOING GOOD.

GALATIANS 6:9

D-DAY FOR THE FAMILY

For where your treasure is, there will your heart be also.

MATTHEW 6:21

Today we need men and women who have the courage to do two things. First, *men and women need the courage to choose real family values*. They need the strength to make godly choices. The historian and essayist Thomas Carlyle wrote, "Conviction is worthless unless it converts itself into conduct." Courage begins at home with what we impart to our children. We need to leave our children a heritage of godly values, not merely an inheritance. And it won't be achieved if we pour our lives into our careers, our pleasure and our hobbies. That heritage is secured only by making our relationships with our children a priority in our lives.

It takes courage to live by priorities. As the verse above reminds us, your heart is where your treasure is. Have you ever thought of your children being treasures worth fighting for?

Second, *men and women need to step out of the safety of their homes and decide to storm the beach* in the same way those brave soldiers stormed the beaches of Normandy on D-day back in 1944. The beach represents territory that is controlled by the enemy. I believe God has a beach for every Christian willing to follow Him. As you walk with God and grow closer to Him, you will begin to see areas of your city that need to be reclaimed for Jesus Christ. Maybe it's a family in your neighborhood. Perhaps it's the school your children attend or associates at work who are ruining their lives with ungodly choices.

I think back to the lieutenant on Omaha Beach on D-day who, along with a wounded sergeant, exposed himself to gunfire to inspect an entanglement of barbed wire that blocked their progress. On his belly he slithered back to his men and asked, "Are you going to lie there and get killed or get up and do something about it?" When nobody moved, he and the sergeant—still under enemy fire—blew up the barbed wire themselves.

What will be said of us when we die? Will we be remembered for courageously upholding biblical values at home and in our communities? The next generation hangs in the balance of your choices and mine. Most of us know what to do. We just need the courage to do it.

Discuss: In what areas of your life has God revealed that you need to make courageous choices?

Pray: Pray that He would press you into battle. Also ask God for an army of lay lieutenants to enlist in the battle for the family so that America's homes might be rebuilt around Jesus Christ—one family at a time.

A VISION FOR YOUR FAMILY

Who is the man who fears the LORD? He will instruct
him in the way he should choose.

PSALM 25:12

Author and poet Antoine de Saint-Exupery once wrote,
"Love does not consist in gazing at each other but in looking outward together in the same direction." Many
Christian families today lack a sense of unified purpose and,
instead of turning outward, are turning inward—not toward
one another, but toward self. Instead of having an impact on
the world, they blend in. Instead of cutting across the grain
of the culture, they go with the flow.

Conformity leads to compromise. Compromise leads to
mediocrity. Mediocrity leads to sin and a wasted life. Finally,
a wasted life leads to a lost legacy.

Determining your life's true direction requires developing a sixth sense: the sense of faith. Through faith you first
begin to grasp the unseen. I have two suggestions for help-
ing you see by faith God's direction. First, *look to the past.*
What causes ideas to surface in your thinking and conversa-

tion? What injustice makes you angry? What burdens your heart about your town, your state or your world?

Barbara and I did not arrive at our present field of ministry overnight. Initially, we ministered to high school students. But during those years we often observed that young people's spiritual growth was negatively affected by the divorce of their parents. This eventually gave us the conviction to help start what is now FamilyLife.

Second, *inventory your talents and gifts*. What unique skills and training has God provided for you? In what specific ways has He used you to influence other people for Christ?

As you think over these issues, pray that God would develop within you a conviction of where He is leading you.

Discuss: Spend some time talking about the two issues just described: How has God led you in the past? What are your burdens and passionate causes? What are your talents and gifts?

Pray: Ask God to begin to "instruct [you] in the way [you] should choose."

DETERMINING YOUR LIFE'S
TRUE DIRECTION REQUIRES
DEVELOPING A SIXTH SENSE:
THE SENSE OF FAITH.

TAKING A STAND

*For I am not ashamed of the gospel, for it is the power of
God for salvation to everyone who believes.*

ROMANS 1:16

One fall day I felt a big lump in my throat as our kids left
early for school. Ashley, age 17; Benjamin, 15; and Samuel,
13, were going to participate in See You at the Pole, a nation-
wide movement of Christian junior and senior high school
students gathering around their schools' flagpoles to pray
for their schools.

The previous evening our family had seen a video pro-
moting See You at the Pole. We had been thrilled to watch as
250 teenagers prayed around their flagpole. We applauded
the courage of a group of only five students who dared to
pray around their school's flagpole while the rest of the student body went their separate ways. But I got a catch in my
throat when the video showed one girl by the pole at another school—she stood alone, praying.

Ashley and Benjamin knew of at least a dozen students
who were planning to pray with them at their high school.
But Samuel knew of only two other students who might
pray with him—and even that wasn't a sure thing. *What if he's
the only one?* I thought.

I looked down at my son through tear-filled eyes. Everything within me wanted to spare him the pain of what he might face. But I realized this was a time for Samuel to count the cost of what it means to be a follower of Christ.

Well, as it turned out, nearly 50 kids out of a student body of 425 showed up to pray with Samuel. God used that event to teach all of us some important lessons. Barbara and I realized our kids need the opportunity to hammer out their own faith in the midst of their doubts, *just like we did*. And it reminded me to take a courageous and public stand for Christ and not be ashamed!

Discuss: Tell about a time when you and your children had the opportunity to take a public stand for Christ. Share a recent time when you were ashamed to stand up for Jesus Christ.

Pray: Ask God to help you and each member of your family never to be intimidated or ashamed to affirm Christian values in a non-Christian world.

LAUNCHING OUR ARROWS

Prove yourselves to be blameless and innocent, children of God above reproach in the midst of a crooked and perverse generation, among whom you appear as lights in the world.

PHILIPPIANS 2:15

During the year after we launched our first child out on her own, Barbara and I notched the bowstring with another arrow, Benjamin, and prepared for our second release (see Ps. 127:4, in which children are described as "arrows"). We spent a lot of time talking to him about the temptations he would encounter at the university. Over breakfast Bible studies we discussed drinking, peer pressure, dating, girls and sex.

Some of these talks had begun when Benjamin was in fifth and sixth grade. Any good archer will tell you that you don't prepare for hunting season by practicing for a couple of weeks right before it begins.

In August, just days before Benjamin was to leave for college, I set up a surprise breakfast for him. We were joined by three godly men whom Benjamin respected. It was powerful!

They encouraged Benjamin to grow in his love for Jesus Christ, to guard his heart and to be faithful to God.

Finally the day came. Arriving on campus, we spent most of the afternoon cleaning our son's room so that he could move in.

It was nearly dusk when the first poignant moment came. Benjamin and I went outside the student housing for some fresh air and sat on the tailgate of a truck parked near the front door. There we watched a steady stream of young men pass by, most of them drinking.

At this point I was becoming fearful for my son. I wanted to protect my arrow and put it back in the quiver, not releasing it into this "crooked and perverse generation." I turned to Benjamin and looked him in the eye. "Son, I've got to tell you that watching all these young men get wasted on booze really causes me to question the wisdom of sending you into the midst of all this."

There was only a brief silence and then he returned my gaze. "Dad, this is my mission field," he replied. "It's going to be tough, but if it were easy, these guys wouldn't need Jesus Christ. This is what you and Mom have trained me for. God has led me here and He will protect me."

There I sat, rebuked by my 18-year-old son. He was a young man of faith.

Discuss: How many years do you have before you release your "arrows"? How are you preparing them for spiritual battle?

Pray: Pray that your children will desire to impact their peers with the love and power of Jesus Christ.

Are You Compelled?

And seeing the multitudes, He felt compassion
for them, because they were distressed and downcast
like sheep without a shepherd.

M A T T H E W   9 : 3 6

I struggle as much as anyone with how to turn a conversation to spiritual things. However, I can't escape a few truths that lead me to step out in faith. First, *I am compelled by the realization that without Christ all men and women are lost and without hope.* Sure, humans do good things, but that doesn't change the fact that we all sin naturally. I've never taught a single one of our six children how to steal a cookie, yet they all have done it. It's part of their sin nature. And it's because of sin that all men and women are lost.

Second, *I'm compelled to share Christ with others because of the reality of hell.* Thinking about hell is not in vogue today. But Christ spoke of hell as a real place of eternal judgment and torment.

Third, *I want to share the good news because it is the very reason for which Christ came to the planet Earth.* Jesus Christ didn't go to the cross just so we could have happy homes. He came "to seek and to save that which was lost" (Luke 19:10).

Look around you. The army of God needs fresh troops who are willing to get into the trenches. The hour couldn't be more urgent. And your family is an important part of the solution.

"So what do I do?" you ask. Below are a few ideas. Don't let this list overwhelm you. The important thing is to start somewhere—with something.

- Read the book *Witnessing Without Fear* by Bill Bright, founder of Campus Crusade for Christ. It will show you how to share your faith with confidence in any type of witnessing situation.
- Have an evangelistic dinner party at your home for a few couples you know.
- Host a Good News Club for neighborhood children.
- Pick up several copies of "The Four Spiritual Laws" at your local Christian bookstore, and use them to explain the gospel.
- Show your children how to share their faith. Invite a neighborhood child to go to church with you.

Now is the time for boldness. Step out and ask people about their relationship with God.

Discuss: Take a few minutes to identify people you know who need Christ. Make a list.

Pray: Ask God to give you an opportunity to share the gospel with them.

THE ARMY OF GOD
NEEDS FRESH TROOPS WHO
ARE WILLING TO GET INTO
THE TRENCHES.

DARE TO RISK

*Thou hast also given me the shield of Thy salvation, and Thy
right hand upholds me; and Thy gentleness makes me great.*

PSALM 18:35

What is the real need among Christians today? It's not
safety, security or a fat savings account. It is not better facil-
ities, better programs, flashier television shows, a celebrity's
testimony, more people in the ministry or an open door for
the gospel in a closed country. These are all needs. But what
is the real need?

Dawson Trotman, founder of the Navigators, was asked
about the need of the hour. He replied,

> I believe in an army of soldiers, dedicated to Jesus
> Christ, who believe not only that He is God but that
> He can fulfill every promise He has ever made, and
> that there isn't anything too hard for Him. It is the
> only way we can accomplish the thing that is on His
> heart—getting the Gospel to every creature.[1]

The real need is for risk takers—those who dare to lean
out over the cliff's edge on the promises of His Word. Jesus

called them disciples. I can assure you I'm a novice, but if I keep going out over the edge, sooner or later I'm going to become a veteran in the faith.

Stepping out in faith doesn't have to be knee jarring, heart pounding or spectacular. For some it may mean volunteering to teach Sunday School or giving additional finances to accomplish the Lord's work. But for others the hazards may be more costly, such as witnessing to a boss or a neighbor. The risk includes the exposure that comes from attempting something that can be pulled off only in and through Jesus Christ.

Venture out! Don't play it safe. Life is too short. Remember Helen Keller's words: "Life is either a daring adventure or nothing." Find your true safety in Christ and go for it!

Discuss: What risk would you take if you knew you could not fail?

Pray: If you don't have a vision for your life and marriage, why not get on your knees tonight as a couple and ask God to help you see what He wants you to do?

Note

1. Dawson Trotman, *The Need of the Hour* (Colorado Springs, CO: The Navigators, 1999), pp. 7-8.

S ince attending a FamilyLife Conference, the Millers have been too distracted to read their favorite books ...

another love story has their attention.

Get away for a romantic weekend together ...

or join us for a life-changing, one-day conference!

For more information or to receive a free brochure, call **1-800-FL-TODAY** (1-800-358-6329), 24 hours a day, or visit **www.familylife.com**

FamilyLife has been bringing couples the wonderful news of God's blueprints for marriage since 1976.

Today we are strengthening hundreds of thousands of homes each year in the United States and around the world through:

- **Weekend to Remember**™ conferences

- **I Still Do**® conferences

- **HomeBuilders Couples Series**® small-group Bible studies

- **"FamilyLife Today,"** our daily, half-hour radio program, and four other nationally syndicated broadcasts

- A comprehensive Web site, **www.familylife.com**, featuring marriage and parenting tips, daily devotions, conference information, and a wide range of resources for strengthening families

- Unique marriage and family **connecting resources**

Through these outreaches, FamilyLife is effectively developing godly families who reach the world one home at a time.

FAMILYLIFE™
Bringing Timeless Principles Home

Dennis Rainey, Executive Director
1-800-FL-TODAY (358-6329)
www.familylife.com

A division of Campus Crusade for Christ